GOD
101

HOW TO MEET GOD
FACE TO FACE

BY
THE CHAPLAIN

[signature]

2 - 2 - 2003

Essence
PUBLISHING

Belleville, Ontario, Canada

God 101

Copyright © 2003, Clare Weakley

Scripture quotations are from the *Revised Standard Version* of the Bible (Copyright © 1946, 1952; © 1971, 1973 by the Division of Christian Education of the National Council of the Churches of Christ in the United States of America.)

The Holy Bible, King James Version. Copyright © 1977, 1984, Thomas Nelson Inc., Publishers.

National Library of Canada Cataloguing in Publication

Chaplain
      God 101 : how to meet God face to face / the Chaplain.

ISBN 1-55306-455-0.—ISBN 1-55306-477-1 (LSI ed.)

      1. God. 2. Christian life. I. Title.

BT103.C44 2002	231	C2002-905838-4

Essence Publishing is a Christian Book Publisher dedicated to furthering the work of Christ through the written word. For more information, contact: 44 Moira Street West, Belleville, Ontario, Canada K8P 1S3.
Phone: 1-800-238-6376. Fax: (613) 962-3055.
E-mail: info@essencegroup.com
Internet: www.essencegroup.com

Printed in Canada
by

Essence
PUBLISHING

To Jesus, who makes this possible.

TABLE OF CONTENTS ·····················

PREFACE ···

All people realize that when this life on earth ends, questions about God will also end. Prudent people want these questions answered now. Discovering the answer later could bring long-lasting and unwanted consequences.

For many, it seems there is no answer to the question, "Does God exist?" God, conceding He exists, is a Spirit and is invisible. Earthly means of meeting and communicating do not apply.

If God exists and wants people to seriously consider Him, He must prove Himself. That is necessary because all are born ignorant of Him and separated from Him.

So in a manner of speaking, we are born lost—lost to God's presence and reality. Since we are lost, God must come find us because He wants us to be found. Fortunately, He will come to find us when we decide we want to be found. Do you want to be found, or do you prefer to stay lost?

There is a simple way to be found. First, you must realize you are lost. Next, you must understand that you are lost and want to be found. Then, you must ask to be found. Once found, you need to agree to follow Him wherever He leads.

If you really want to be in God's presence and be assured you have been found, read *GOD 101*. Seriously consider its thoughts, and God will show Himself to you.

INTRODUCTION ··

If there is a *True Religion*, it must have universal appeal and universal application. That is, *True Religion* must apply to all people, at all places, and at all times, regardless of age, sex, education, race, or place. All people, in all places and times, must be able to understand and enjoy personal faith.

Examine the various *religious systems* that are commonly called religions. None qualify as religion. All require special acts and beliefs that cannot be universally applied. *True Religion* is not simply membership in some religious system or institution. Religion is a personal relationship with God. For this, we need to meet God directly.

Many may discuss God, but that is simply an intellectual exercise. Nothing short of God's personal touch satisfies our soul. Religious systems can only describe God's visit. They cannot give God's visit. We want and need heart-felt faith given by God's loving grace.

Our yearning for God's power and presence in all of life's events is satisfied only when God touches our minds and hearts. All God requires from us is a desire to have Him as our daily companion. Although we seek this companionship, we can be bewildered and distracted by the many religious systems. Let *GOD 101* remove confusion, and simplify your spiritual journey.

NOTES

ENTRY ···

The purpose of *GOD 101* is to guide you into a personal meeting with God. The course contents contain material to induce discussion about the nature of God. However, those who mistake our goal of meeting God face-to-face, with simply discussing God, will miss the point of the book.

Hopefully, you will be able to set aside preconceived ideas or denominational bias during this study. An open mind allows new investigation into the reality and presence of the living God. This study should bring the inquirer to an infilling with God's (Holy) Spirit and His power. When you have a personal experience of God's actual and daily presence in your life, you have an everlasting guarantee of His reality and eternal love.

Requirements from participants are minimal. God will do most of the work for your success in this study. This book may be read as slowly as you wish. It is designed to have space to note your observations as you read. A New Testament translation of your choice may be helpful in improving your understanding of this material. However, extra Bible reading is not the goal of this study. The goal remains that of stimulating your thinking about the nature and presence of a personal living God.

GOD 101 is designed for self-study. You are encouraged to take as much time as you wish. There is no hurry for you to get to the end of this book. If you need additional insight, inspiration, or understanding please contact the course counselor. Appendix A provides counselor information.

NOTES

PROOF ··

Ninety-six percent of the American people believe in God or a higher power. The other four percent are on their own. For seventy years, the U.S.S.R. tried life without God. Their results are open for inspection. There is no reason to think any other atheist is any more correct than the Communists. We will move on assuming that God is. Proof will come later.

It is not possible for God to ever love anyone more than He already loves you. Next, it is impossible for you to do anything to make God change His love for you. Whatever you do, good or bad, God loves you as much as He ever has or ever will love anyone. Until you have a face-to-face meeting with God, you don't have much reason to seriously believe this.

Simply saying God exists will not make you feel good. Neither will it improve your daily living. We all must confront the great truth about God: simply knowing about God is not the same as knowing Him. Many have studied ideas about God. Only a few want to go beyond study and meet Him face-to-face.

Lengthy Bible studies, memorization of Bible verses, extended church activity, familiarity with religious characters and religious history, ordination into the ministry, and theology degrees are no substitute for a personal encounter with God.

If knowing about God is not the same as knowing God, how do we get introduced? We must face another great fact. Only God Himself can prove His reality. Works and reason cannot prove that God exists. He reserves that proof for Himself. God proves His reality by showing Himself. When God kisses your soul and plants His Spirit in you, you know He is real.

God loves you. You can meet God face-to-face. You can do it now. So what? How will that improve your daily living? Will God solve your problems and make your life simpler and easier? Can God intervene in your daily affairs? If so, how?

14

NOTES

DEFINITION ···

What is God's occupation? What is God doing? Is God working in your life or just standing back watching you?

An age old discussion is how God acts in our lives. This continuing dispute concerns *deism* as opposed to *theism*. Deists believe God created all things, but doesn't intervene in human affairs. Theists believe there is a God who is alive, awake, and He can and will move in our lives—for better or worse.

In Jesus' time, Sadducees were deists and Pharisees were theists. In those days, Pharisees disputed among themselves about what actions were necessary to win God's favor. The trick then, as now, was to figure what we could do to persuade God to answer our requests and supply our needs, assuming God was persuadable.

The Old Testament records Jewish understanding of God's acts toward their people and in their nation. Listed there are six hundred and thirteen laws to be followed. Jewish teachers—rabbis—decided how these Torah laws should be applied in life. The Rabbinical interpretations, now called Mishnah and Talmud, were the traditions Jesus loathed (Mark 7:1-23). Those were personal interpretations of Torah creating rituals and works that effectively changed the "laws".

Each of us has our own "tradition" about God's nature, the way God acts, and what pleases or displeases Him. What is yours? What do you think you must do to please God?

Can you simply state your idea of God and how He works in not more than twenty words? One dictionary definition of God is: "The Being perfect in power, wisdom, and goodness whom men worship as creator and ruler of the universe."

What does this say about God's love or His works? Does it say enough? Think about each word used. What does "ruler" mean? Think about *perfect power, wisdom, goodness*, and *creator*. Can you apply these words to your God?

NOTES

YOU ··

Now you know what you think about God. What do you suppose God thinks about you? Can you write that in twenty words?

This is not a popular question. Imagining what God thinks about us is not our most sought after thrill. In the past, our primary efforts were directed toward keeping God at bay.

Responses to this question run from one extreme to the other. On one end a few say, "I have been so bad, God could never accept me. Surely God has turned my portrait toward the wall. There is little for me to write, and I can put that into four words: I am too bad!"

At the other extreme are a few who insist they have never done anything really wrong. "After all," they confide, "I have never been in jail. Surely God thinks I am O.K. I can write that with only three words: I am fine."

In the middle, many think, "I do the best I can. What more could God expect? Lots of people live lives worse than me. I am sure He accepts me as I am. In two words I say: I try."

The most common belief is that God judges us by our acts and our behavior. But, we imagine the good works necessary to fully please God will take too much attention and effort. To many, living with both eyes on God seems irrelevant, foolish, detrimental to happiness, and unnecessarily stressful.

Regardless of our self-image, none of us want to have our secrets reviewed on the front page of our local newspaper. We have all done some things that are embarrassing. God knows about those events. We imagine those events are the basis of what God thinks about us. So why hurry to read His list?

We suppose that someday, sometime in the future, we will consider God's opinion more seriously. Until then we say, "Lets get on with the business at hand. There are decisions to make, bills to pay, and fun to be had. Because God knows me, He understands how busy I am. He will forgive me."

18

NOTES

ATTENTION ···

God does know you are busy. God can wait until you are ready to have a face-to-face relationship. But can you wait? Do you know what you are missing? While you wait, you miss the blessings God has planned for you from your beginning.

You are not an accident of nature. God was not surprised when you were born. You were planned from the first day of creation. God knew when you would be here, where you would be, and what you would need to fulfill your particular life plan. He would like to start working with you on your plan, but He cannot without your approval and cooperation.

To get your cooperation, He must get your attention. There are two ways to gain your notice. One is the hard way, the other is the easy way. The hard way is waiting until life has become unbearable before asking for His help. The easy way is to seek God's companionship because that is the wisest choice.

That wise choice is wise because simple logic tells us God is smarter than we are. Assuming God is real and loves us more than we love ourselves, cooperation is the only sensible choice. Given God's brains and His love, He will always do a better job of managing your life than you can do on your own.

Yet the prime problem remains. Unless God comes to meet you personally, God talk is only theological speculation. Who can understand an invisible principle? Where is the proof? We need proof that the invisible God is both real and theistic.

Fortunately, God knows the problem and has a quick and simple solution. He will bring the proof to you. You do not have to learn and keep six hundred and thirteen laws. You do not have to have a clean record. A theological education is unnecessary. You do not need any religious or magical words or rituals. You do not need a saint to intervene for you. All you have to do is ask God to take over your life.

NOTES

SIMPLICITY ···

How many religions, faiths, and denominations do you think there are in the world today? Can you guess? Maybe fifty-thousand? How many do you suppose there have been since the beginning of humanity? Twenty percent more? Guess a number.

Don't ask me. I don't know. I do know this. No matter how great the number of established religions, each is modified by personal beliefs. Simply, there are as many religions as there are people. Everyone has their particular ideas about religion and about God. So, how can you know which is right?

Jesus' religion was Judaism, minus its invented traditions. Judaism was His religion because He was a Jew in Israel. He was called to do a particular mission to the Jews, at a particular time. Note though, He debated with His religious teachers and leaders. He applied His right to think as He chose. It cost Him His life, but to the end He stuck to His principle. Can you follow His example to think for yourself?

What did Jesus believe until death? He believed you could and should have a direct relationship with God. He wanted you to know how much God loves you. He thought you needed to know that God will always take care of you. He wanted you to know God personally, face-to-face. He wanted to remove the many religious ideas, rituals and formulas that do not do anything to increase God's love for you or His presence in your life.

His simple truth is that faith is a relationship, not a statement, or only an intellectual exercise. Jesus said our route to God is so simple even a little child could touch God now and for eternity. Jesus wanted to give you a simple statement of that faith that no one could change. He did it. He gave you "The Lord's Prayer" to be your creed in all times under all conditions. It belongs to you. Now, let's examine that treasure and see why it is almost universally revered.

NOTES

CREED ···

"The Lord's Prayer," is a non-threatening meeting place for people of all religious beliefs. It is not unusual to see, or be in, a group of people of various faiths reciting Jesus' prayer. Often these people, both cold and warm on religion, will hold hands in a prayer circle while speaking the prayer.

Isn't this interesting? Religious discussions can become so testy that they are banned in many work places. Yet, this simple prayer brings harmony instead of dissension, agreement instead of debate. This portion of Jesus' "Sermon On The Mount" is found in Matthew 6:6-13:

"But when ye pray, use not vain repetitions, as the heathen do: for they think that they shall be heard for their much speaking. Be not ye therefore like unto them: for your Father knoweth what things ye have need of, before ye ask him. After this manner therefore pray ye:

Our Father which art in heaven, Hallowed be thy name. Thy kingdom come, Thy will be done in earth, as it is in heaven. Give us this day our daily bread. And forgive us our debts, as we forgive our debtors. And lead us not into temptation, but deliver us from evil: For thine is the kingdom, and the power, and the glory, for ever. Amen."

Too often we ignore Jesus' warning about endless and empty phrases. Missing the truth about this prayer, we repeat it thoughtlessly as if the words alone are magic and will somehow please God. Believing that His hearing us say these words pleases Him, we think, "Surely I am religious because I pray in public."

If you think this prayer motivates God, you miss the relationship God offers you. He doesn't need to hear the prayer because He created it. We need to hear what God is saying to us from it. Next, let's examine the words and find the promises God gave us in this comfortable and familiar prayer. It is our statement of faith, our creed, our treasure of truth.

24

NOTES

FATHER ··

"Our Father" reminds us that God is creator and is everyone's father. All people are His children and in His family, so mankind is a brotherhood. We have heard that thesis from our earliest memories. Do we act as if we really believe it?

If there is such a brotherhood of mankind, it operates under the Cain and Abel syndrome. There is little brotherly love and much sibling rivalry. Person to person competition, even for parking slots, is intense and often violent.

The brotherhood of mankind in this prayer is not Jesus' main theme. In the Lord's Prayer, you are confirming a real live God as *your* Father. Anything less ignores the potency of this opening statement. The God of all creation is *your* Father. But what does Father mean in this prayer?

In Jesus' times, both in the East (Oriental world) and the West (Greco-Roman world) the father totally controlled his family. The father owned all the property and made all the decisions. The children were always subject to the father's supervision. In return, the father provided all the children with protection and prosperity. His duty was to protect his children from want.

While family members had their father's love and support, they could leave the family. Those who left the family were on their own without any of their father's support. Once gone, they would continue to have their father's love but ceased to have his presence, power, prestige, or wealth.

Do you live in your Father's house, under His love and protection, or are you living out on your own?

NOTES

WHERE ···

"Which art in heaven." In the New Testament, Jesus used both the Kingdom of Heaven and the Kingdom of God to mean the same thing. He said this Kingdom is here, now. What? What does that mean? How do you "go to heaven" if heaven is here, now?

He was talking about the spiritual nature of existence. You have an inner spirit (pneuma), given to you when you were created. Pneuma is your life and being, that spark that energizes you and makes you a person. Without pneuma (spirit), you would be a non-person corpse. That fact should confirm that life depends on spirit. Logic should remind us that because life depends on spirit, spirit comes first and then material follows.

Believe it or not, the spiritual realm of existence governs all material manifestations. Because the spiritual is invisible and the material is visible, our concepts get turned upside down. We believe what we do here, in the material, motivates and moves the spiritual realm. Simply, we believe our words, works, and thoughts control events. It never occurs to us that spirits control our thoughts that end in our words, and acts.

We should have a better grip on logic than this. We know God is Spirit. We know God is everywhere. We believe God knows everything. We think God is all powerful. Then we park our brains and live as deists. We act as if God cannot or will not work in our lives here on earth, at this material level.

In this portion of Jesus' prayer/creed, we try to bring our brains back to reality. God is in heaven. Heaven is spiritual. God is in control. When we are controlled by God's spirit, we are with Him. Then we are in the Kingdom of God—the Kingdom of Heaven. His Spirit is loosed in us to pilot our lives. This is reality, life as it is.

NOTES

HOLY ··

"Hallowed be thy name." Hallowed is an early English word that means sanctified. We prefer translating it "holy" as if there were some common understanding of that word's meaning. Just for fun, define holy. It may be easier to say what holy isn't than what holy is. How are you doing on it?

If we say this phrase in Jesus' prayer/creed, we are making both an abstract statement and a personal confession. We are not just throwing God a bone to placate Him. He does not need to hear compliments or have adulation. God already knows who He is without our descriptions of His person. He doesn't need to have us fawn at His feet.

So our abstract statement that God is holy doesn't help Him. It helps us focus our attention on the Father's nature. At the intellectual level, your definition declares Him holy. Now what do you really think? Is He holy according to your feelings? Do you treat God as if He is holy? Do you speak about God as if He is an important part of life? Do you talk about him at all?

If, in your mind, God is the holy God of all things, and your heavenly Father, you will venerate Him, worship Him, and want to consider Him in all your decisions. You will have a deep, heartfelt love for Him. Do you, or is God just as abstract to you as is the word holy?

If you have never met God face-to-face, you can't revere Him. How can you love and revere someone you have never met? How can you revere someone you are not sure exists? You can't. You really need to meet this Father but He must introduce Himself to you. No one else can take His place doing that.

NOTES

KINGDOM ···

"Thy Kingdom come." We know that the Kingdom of God is His Spirit in our hearts. *"The Kingdom of God is within you"*, so said Jesus (Luke 17:21). But what does it mean to be in God's kingdom? What will happen in your life? Should you really be praying for this to happen? Do you really want this?

Now we are headed toward serious religion. This acknowledges that God has a plan and we want it put into effect. Until now, we were simply discussing the nature of God and his program. We are now asking Him to put His program into effect. Can we justify taking this radical step? Easily done!

Common sense tells us that if everyone lived under God's "Golden Rule" and in "brotherly love," there would not be any man-made problems in the world. There wouldn't be any need for police, defense budgets, government regulators, watch dogs, locks, fences, or any program for self-protection. We could cut our taxes and put all efforts into correcting social ills and satisfying individual needs. Family problems would disappear, as would divorce and its consequences.

But if common sense tells us that is a good idea, our selfish interests reject it. We think God has a good plan but does not have the muscle and mind to make it work for "me." So, we must continue to look out for "number one" because God can't, or won't. This works until it doesn't work.

When we really understand that we need God's help in looking out for number one, then we can honestly pray this phrase. This requires an honest step of faith that we haven't exercised before. It requires putting God's needs in front of our needs. We must conclude that God comes first, knows best, can deliver, and that we are no better than second.

NOTES

WILL ··

"Thy will be done." Let me ask you a question. Assuming you are going to the Spirit world—Heaven—after you die, what are you going to do for eternity? Do you know? Have you thought about it? I know what I am going to do in the hereafter Heaven. I am going to do what I am told to do. I am going to do what God tells me to do. I am going to be obedient to His "will".

Doing God's will is a choice, of sorts, in this world. It becomes a necessity in the world to come. The world to come, Heaven, in the hereafter sense, is called "Paradise." Life there, we assume, will be trouble free and always in the presence of God. There we think we will be bathed in God's love, and always be carefree and joyful.

Do you have any reason to dispute that picture of life after death? Maybe you are not sure of what the living conditions will be in that later Heaven, but you know you will not be in control. Don't you? You do know you will need to do what you are told to do. Don't you? I do!

In this prayer phrase, we are agreeing with the inevitable. God's will shall be done because He is God and He has the power to cause anything to happen. Honestly spoken, this phrase is our intellectual commitment to submit to God's will as we can best understand it and conform to it. Here we admit God has a will and we will follow it, if we can figure out how. Instinctively, or at least hopefully, we think God can show us His will.

Now this part of the prayer becomes more than a thoughtless liturgy. It is our acknowledgment that God is real, alive, and has a will. We are agreeing to accept and implement His will. Now we wonder, what is supposed to happen next?

NOTES

HERE ··

"On Earth as in Heaven." Here? Most of us have been told that God wants us to be good—good beyond our ability. We are supposed to do good works and always behave, so we can go to Heaven when we die. So we have been told.

But the truth is we are not really concerned with that right now. We have more to do daily than we can handle. Sure, it is nice to be moral and try to think of God's rules, but presently that is not our main interest, and is far too hard. "As long as we are not breaking the law, please don't rock our boat." God's main will, we say, is for us not to harm others.

God's will for us is something much greater than not harming others. His will for us is to experience all His joy, love, and plenty here on earth, on earth as in heaven. It is to know Him and enjoy His power and presence in our life here, long before our later afterlife. But to get serious about doing His will now, we need to know that He is fully in control.

The major stress in life is solving the daily problems that go with meeting our bodily needs. Most of our time and thought is directed toward our employment. We must know we can pay our bills. Worrying about food, clothing, shelter, and danger detracts from any serious theological speculation. We need assurances about our "daily bread" before we can pay more attention to God.

Jesus, of course, already knew that. So, He assured us, in His prayer, that our daily needs were also subject to God's power and part of His grace package. God's help in those efforts is necessary before we can really get serious about religion. If God doesn't help with our daily needs, we are really still on our own.

36

NOTES

SUPPLY ···

"Give us this day our daily bread." What type of bread does this phrase mean? Sliced or loaf? White, wheat, or rye?

In Jesus' day bread was the main course everyday. It was the most important human food, the essential element for life. *Lechem*, the Hebrew word for food also translates as bread. It appears two hundred and sixty times in the Old Testament. The Greek word for food and bread, used the same way in the New Testament is *artos*. There it appears eighty one times, with Jesus speaking it on twenty-two of those occasions.

Bread really means what we need for our daily sustenance. Without stretching the point, we can rephrase this clause in another way. It is the same as if Jesus taught us to pray, "Give us the money we need to live today." That understanding is so common that in slang, "bread" means money.

We acknowledge in this part of Jesus' prayer that God is involved in our income process. Our Father, in His love, wants to provide our daily sustenance. His will is for us to have the necessary food, clothing, and shelter. His will for us is that all our needs—material and spiritual—shall be met.

God wants to supply our needs so we can keep our attention focused on His total will—what He wants us to do on earth, before we get to heaven. An early promise from Jesus is that our Father gives all necessary gifts, grace, and providence to us when we seek His will and follow it. Matthew 6:25-34 records God's guarantee to be our provider.

When we know these promises are true, and we can rely on God to lead us through our greatest concerns, it is easier to be serious about religion. A real God, who does real things for us which can be seen quickly, gains our attention and respect.

NOTES

FORGIVE

The Lord's Prayer is divided into six couplets. The first teaches about God's nature. The second asks for His will to be done now. The third asks Him to provide for our material needs. Now we are looking at the fourth couplet. It asks Him to forgive our mistakes. The first line of the two is "and forgive us our debts," our trespasses.

There are several dynamics in this short phrase. The first is the admission that we need forgiving. The next is that God has the power to forgive. Also, it assumes God is inclined to forgive. Overall, it is a confession that we are fallible. "Occasionally" we have made some noticeable mistakes.

The petition for forgiveness ties to Jesus' Beatitudes (Matt. 5:1-12). It relates to most of them. For us to admit faults and ask for forgiveness, the key Beatitude attitudes must be felt. To ask for forgiveness, one would be poor in spirit, mourning, meek, searching for righteousness, merciful, seeking purity of heart and also wanting to be a peace maker.

Of course, asking for forgiveness can be done from the fear of expected or deserved divine punishment. However, the prayer doesn't require a particular motive. It just requests God to forgive our mistakes. The fact that we ask God for forgiveness acknowledges His power and primacy.

On a more general basis, here we acknowledge that there is some proper order for all of us. The prayer says, "forgive us our debts." The plural pronoun of *us* implies that all people have fallen short of God's requirements. All are in the same boat.

We have a commonality as humans standing before God. None of us is better than another. If we all have fallen short of God's requirements and need His forgiveness, what are our shortcomings? Do you know yours?

NOTES

HAPPINESS ··

Our shortcomings are the opposites of Jesus' Beatitudes. Instead of blessings and happiness, our shortcomings give us unhappiness. An important Beatitude is the one about peace makers. Peace is synonymous with contentment and happiness. Anger and resentment are the opposites of peace and destroy happiness.

Unhappiness is something we all want to avoid. It is no secret that anger is an unhappy feeling. Unforgiveness and resentment are unhappy feelings. Too often we carry old resentments that keep us unhappy and cause us to make bad decisions.

The problem with that sort of thinking is that you, the victim, continue to be the only person who is hurt. You stay unhappy while the person who hurt you isn't experiencing any of your resentment and anger. You remain an unhappy victim in continuing anger and misery.

Giving up old unhappy feelings is a good reason to forgive. There is an additional reason. You can't be forgiven until you forgive: *"and forgive us our debts"* links with *"as we also have forgiven our debtors."* As the old song line goes, "you can't have one without the other."

The dynamic truth here is that forgiving helps us in two ways. It releases us from unhappiness in our emotions, as well as separation from God. When we forgive, we are open to receive God's blessings. Jesus promised, *"Blessed are the peacemakers, for they shall be called sons of God."*

The Bible is full of God's directions which is a problem for some people. If it were easy to follow God's instructions everyone would be complying. The truth is, it is difficult to even want to forgive. To fulfill this requirement, we need God's help. Fortunately, He gives it. Part of His power package is for Him to do His will in us and for us.

NOTES

GUIDANCE ··

The best deal I can imagine is to be guided by a wise and loving God. Such guidance could eliminate many bad mistakes.

Asking God to lead us in anything is to ask Him for guidance in everything, because life is an uncompartmentalized unit. All things that happen to us tie together. If we want something to occur in our life, that event has before and after consequences with each affecting the other. Once again, "you can't have one without the other."

So to ask God to lead us in one thing, is to ask Him to lead us in all things. Many people do not realize this unity of events when they pray for a favor. So we may ask something from God and complain when He fails to give it, not realizing He could be protecting us from some unwanted consequence.

When we realize life's unity, we understand that if God grants us a specific wish, specific consequences will automatically follow. Those consequences may not be imagined or desired when we first give God the prayer petition. If we always knew the ultimate results, we might never ask the favor.

Now we understand what Jesus meant when He taught us to pray, *"lead us not into temptation."* With these five words, we pray, "Keep me out of bad deals. Do not let me be tempted to want, or do, anything that is not good for me. Do not let me sin against you."

In this prayer phrase, we move from acknowledging that God has a will for us to asking Him to exert His will by leading us. We do that knowing that when we ask Him to lead us in one thing, we are asking Him to lead us in all things.

Here is our commitment to what we earlier affirmed in, *"thy will be done on earth as in heaven."* *"Lead us"* is our new and personal statement of trust in God. We have moved from spoken words to belief and can truly say, "In God we trust."

44

NOTES

RESCUER ···

The second part of this couplet is, "But deliver us from evil." Translated, the word *deliver* can also mean to rescue or to protect. In this prayer line we see two things. First, there are bad things outside of our control that can happen to us. Next, Jesus says that God has the power to protect us from those maladies and bad treatment. Do you agree?

Everyone has uninvited events, both good and bad, which come into their life. Unscientific explanations of the causes are called superstitions. From earliest humans, desire to control events has led people to create ideas about luck and fate. Hoping to control events, people everywhere, and in every time, have invented various human rituals to control life. Those rituals include both words and works. We call such rituals "magic."

In the simple words of His prayer creed, Jesus has gone far beyond primitive superstitions and magic. He has turned our attention to a God who affects events when we ask. Jesus describes a benevolent Father who doesn't need any motivation to get Him moving. He loves us simply because He created us. He protects and provides for His children. He does not need any bribery by primitive magic or religious rituals.

Jesus says we only need to ask. Ask God to deliver us from the mischief, malice, and viciousness that comes to us from the world. We should trust this live, powerful, loving God to deliver us from sin, sinners, and oppression of all sorts.

Jesus was a realist. He knew oppression—both spiritual and material—would come. He never said that it would be fun. He just said, trust God to handle it. He has the power and purpose to prevail for you. And if He seems a bit slow in showing up, trust Him anyhow. He promised your Father's support while you wait. Who else can you call on for help?

NOTES

AFFIRMATION ···

The closing statement of Jesus' prayer and creed is, *"for thine is the kingdom and the power and the glory, forever."* His affirmation of the nature of God—kingdom, power, and glory—stand apart from the last word, forever. So here we talk about God's nature and discuss eternity next.

Early in Jesus' prayer, He prayed that God's kingdom would come on earth, as it is in heaven. We worked on that several pages back. We also admitted that God has the power to do what He wishes, whenever He wishes. Hopefully, we have agreed that God uses His power to give us comfort, peace and security.

So it is duplication to go back into the fact that creation is God's kingdom, designed by Him, functioning according to His purpose. The fact that His purpose may seem strange or incomprehensible to us does not change the fact that God is in charge. It is His kingdom and He has full power. So there is no debate about that.

But why glory? What is God's glory? Glory, as used here, means that God is due honor, praise and worship, but not simply because He is God. It is not very exciting to bow down and glorify God only because He is the creator with full power.

We can glorify and worship God only after we experience Him face-to-face. Once we have a personal meeting with the God of creation, and are touched by His awesome love, we cannot resist calling Him glorious. Then we worship and glorify Him because we personally know Him, His love, majesty, and plan.

When we know we have an eternal security in God and from Him, our fragility and loneliness vanish. That is a glorious experience, so we tell Him our feelings. It is easy to say, Thine is the kingdom and the power and the glory—forever.

NOTES

FOREVER ··

Someone once said that the two longest words in the English language are never and forever. In the King James (Authorized) Version of the Bible, the word forever is divided. There it is rendered for ever. In our time, the two words have become one, but the meaning has not changed.

For ever means what it says. Forever. Perpetual. Time without an end. It is everlasting time with an open end. Endless time is a difficult concept because we have devised ways to measure time's passing. Thus, we have a calendar to measure days, weeks, months, and years. We use clocks to measure minutes and hours of each day. We have divided our calendar into two parts, one before the Christian Era and the other after the Christian Era to better understand large time blocks.

God, Himself, divided time into periods to help people with their work. Days and nights teach us there is a time to work and a time to rest. He gave four seasons, alternating between one for work and another for rest.

Because of our habit of defining time in discernible units, we have no way of understanding eternity—the forever. It doesn't concern us because we don't understand it and cannot do anything about it. Eternity is there. We are in it. We cannot get out. Time is forever and so are we. We are as eternal as creation. It never ends and neither do we.

Have you considered what you are going to be doing forever? Do you know where you will be, and with whom? We know that eternity is out of our control. The next life will be a new experience, probably unlike this one. And, it will be under the power of God, and in His presence.

What will it be like to face God each day while remembering how we acted while on earth? In heaven, God will be taken seriously. There we must do his will without debate or choice. Here we can choose to do His will or ignore it. There, we will have to explain our earthly choices. That is an interesting concept, isn't it?

NOTES

BLESSINGS ··

The New Testament is a record of Jesus' words, works, and legacy. Jesus was God's messenger. His ministry made it possible for you to know God face-to-face. His only mission was to effect this relationship and open God's store house of blessings to you now. It is not necessary to wait for another time, later in your life, to meet God. Now is the time.

The "Sermon on the Mount" is Jesus' first recorded public discourse. The first book of the New Testament is Matthew, where the "Sermon" is preserved in chapters five, six and seven. In it are the two best known lessons Jesus spoke, "The Beatitudes" and "The Lord's Prayer."

God's blessings are promised in each of the nine beatitudes, posted at the first of the "Sermon" in Matthew's chapter five. Each sentence begins with the word, blessed. Our English expression for this condition is beatitude, from the root word, beatify. We define beatify as having attained or received God's blessedness. Thus, "The Beatitudes" tell us that God's blessings are real, and provide great rewards.

Because we live in the material plane of existence, we can think about blessings only at that level. We think that God's blessings are about health, wealth, and protection. But God's blessings are not that limited. His gifts do include supplying our material needs, but extend much further. He gives personal attention, individual spiritual gifts, and faith. He lets you know His reality, love and presence. These are private events between you and your *Father*, so you can get to know Him, and the two of you can enjoy each other.

As you read "The Beatitudes" you see that this attitude is the key to receiving blessings. Nowhere in His teachings does Jesus say your religious works, in church or out, are what causes God to act in your life. The reverse is true. He taught about attitudes. Your attitudes are what direct your acts and make them good or bad. Understanding this will open God's storehouse of blessings to you.

NOTES

HEAVEN ···

The first Beatitude blessing promise is to the poor in spirit. *"Blessed are the poor in spirit: for theirs is the Kingdom of Heaven"* (Matt. 5:3). The Kingdom of Heaven is here, now, as opposed to some hereafter place. "The Kingdom of God," Jesus said, "is within you." Jesus' promise is that the poor in spirit will enter heaven while still living on earth.

This requirement has an unpleasant sound. No one likes the idea of being poor. Balanced against the negative of the word poor, is the idea of heaven's grandness. A paradox?

True, poor means being without. Further, in Jesus' times the poor had nothing. They were destitute, paupers, beggars who were dependent on others. This beatitude says you are to be devoid of spirit so you can become totally dependent on God. What a contrast to modern life. You have been taught to be reasoning, independent, self-sufficient, and proud.

You will rebel at this idea unless you understand the words "poor" and "spirit" and tie them together. Spirit, or *pneuma*, is the energy of life. Simply, spirit means you, your personality as you are, and as you function. Your spirit includes your attitude about yourself and life.

Jesus' message here is that when you become small in your own eyes, you are ready to depend on God for your blessings. This is easy to understand. As long as you remain *rich* in spirit you are self-sufficient and never imagine that you need God. You manage your life and make your choices all alone.

Only after you realize that your efforts are not providing the inner satisfaction you crave can you develop this poverty of spirit attitude. When you admit your limitations, God can move in with you, bring you into His presence, the Kingdom of Heaven, and begin blessing your life.

NOTES

REPENT ··

The second beatitude pivots around another word with negative connotations. *"Blessed are they that mourn: for they shall be comforted"* (Matt. 5:4). Mourning usually carries the idea of survivors grieving after a death. But here *mourn* has a different meaning.

Broadly speaking, mourning is the emotion of sadness. In this beatitude Jesus puts value on sadness. Sadness, He says, will bring blessings. What type of sadness? In the first beatitude, you were instructed to become humble, small in your own eyes, and start intensely relying on God.

To get to that point, you reviewed your past and found it lacking. Past decisions and experiences have not brought the joy and hope you wanted. Looking back at those mistakes brings unspoken regrets, "If only...." These regrets are the sadness, the mourning, of this beatitude.

Your sadness about what has been lost—confidence, peace, joy, and hope—led you to the broken spirit of the first beatitude. Your brokenness gave you a changed attitude about God. Now it turns you to a changed attitude about life. True mourning is regretting past sins, damage done to others, and time wasted ignoring God. The result can be self-pity, stoic endurance, or resolution to seek change.

Resolving to change your ideas and attitude is repentance. It is both turning away from the past and turning toward a new beginning. When you do this, God promises to bless you. He will actually come to you, comfort you, and let you feel His love.

Forgiveness removes guilt. This is both the blessing and the comfort. When God puts His love into your heart, He lets you know you are forgiven. Your guilt for all your sins and mistakes is instantly removed. You are comforted, you are blessed, and you know God is real.

NOTES

MEEK ··

Here in the third beatitude, again there is a word that gives some negative feelings. *"Blessed are the meek: for they shall inherit the earth"* (Matt. 5:5). On first glance, meek implies weakness. A popular idea of a meek person is one who lacks spirit and courage. A second look at the dictionary yields other and more positive definitions.

The meek is one who is strong but not violent, able to endure injury with patience and without resentment. A better idea of the meaning is "humility." The meek person of this beatitude is one who is secure, humble, and unassuming. Jesus called Himself meek and gentle. It describes a person who is able to handle conflicts and insults without an ego crisis. In our time, we say the meek person is one who "has it all put together."

Jesus said these non-aggressors would inherit the earth. What did he mean? Inheritance is to receive an unearned gift. The recipient is an heir who, without personal effort, takes control and ownership of property as a beneficiary. This idea contrasts with the popular belief that you *must* work harder, think faster, and compete aggressively to succeed.

But it is here—the meek shall inherit the earth. What is the earth? Here *earth* means the realm of your existence. It is your environment. It is the place and circumstance of your life.

So the humble and gentle will be given control of their existence. God will do this. He will cause harmony between the meek and all the circumstances of their lives. Toil and effort to exist, survive, and succeed are no longer required. The God who controls all things takes control of your life to make your efforts easier, more productive and satisfying.

Strife can become a thing of the past when your life is in God's hands, and is managed by His power and love. Worry and anxiety go away. This is His gift, His blessing to the meek.

NOTES

RIGHTEOUS ···

"Blessed are those who hunger and thirst for righteousness, for they shall be satisfied" (Matt. 5:6).

Everyone imagines that their motives are pure. Ask anyone why they made a particular choice and they will always give a righteous reason. You have never heard anyone say, "I did that just to be mean, ugly, and stupid."

It would be good to look back over our past and say our actions are always blameless and full of good intentions. You already know we can't. You faced that issue two pages ago at the mourning beatitude.

Doing any dumb, angry, or revengeful act is painful in two ways. First, it is terribly embarrassing for your mistakes to show up in public. Next, bad results always come from bad acts. So you need to make righteous choices that translate into moral acts for your own sake. It makes life easier.

But that doesn't always happen. The truth is that most of us are as Paul described himself in his letter to the Romans. "I do not control my own actions. I do not do what I want, but do what I would not." Guilt and damage caused by this quirk of human nature makes your soul "hunger and thirst" for right choices and habitual righteousness.

Hungering is a discomfort caused by lack of necessary nutrients. Thirsting is a strong need for life sustaining fluid. Hungering and thirsting puts all other needs into the back of your mind. "I must," you say, "get something to eat and drink, now!"

Built into us is a hunger to be right. We want to be seen as righteous. Righteousness is the food and drink of our spiritual health. It makes us comfortable. To be complete, we must be righteous: free from guilt, shame, and sin.

Being made righteous is to be set upright and in conformity with God's laws. You can depend on God's promise to grow His righteousness in you.

NOTES

MERCY ···

No doubt the most popular short prayer in every culture is, "God have mercy." Even when abbreviated simply to "God," or sometimes "Oh, God," our petition is the same. We ask God to be merciful with us, and hope He will. This prayer expresses our natural human belief that God is merciful and "will have mercy on whom He will have mercy."

Mercy is a compassionate attitude toward others, with a desire to alleviate their discomfort or distress. In times of disaster, compassion and concern for the distress of others seems to be our natural and normal behavior. In such times many will put aside their personal interests and work for the common good as best they can. Some might say Jesus' mercy beatitude is unnecessary because we have some internal drive for compassion.

A close look at mankind's history proves the opposite. Man's inhumanity to man has always been the ruling force of history. The tragic story of our past is selfishness, inconsideration, and cruelty. The continual result is political oppression, war, poverty, and slavery. General indifference to social distress has generated mandatory government welfare programs addressing every human need.

So our core nature is not generous mercy but self-concern and indifference. In this fifth beatitude, Jesus tied giving mercy with receiving mercy. Here you are told God's rule is for mercy, and the more mercy you give, the more you will receive. That has always been a spiritual law: as you sow, so shall you reap (Gal. 6:7).

God's will for you is a merciful attitude that will bring about merciful acts. He promises His mercy to you. He asks you to be as merciful to others as you want Him to be merciful to you. *"Blessed are the merciful: for they shall obtain mercy"* (Matt. 5:7). Mercy is marvelous. Mercy brings its own rewards.

NOTES

PURITY ···

No doubt, the least visited discussion topic is purity. Can you remember the last time you had a good conversation about it? Think about radio and television talk shows. Have any of those dedicated a show to this subject? And what about church sermons? Can you recall a good window-rattling sermon on purity and its cause and effect?

Jesus wanted us to consider purity. So the sixth beatitude of His sermon is, *"Blessed are the pure in heart: for they shall see God"* (Matt. 5:8). The very reason He wanted us to think about purity is why we would rather not. Purity takes some mental concentration and dedication. He wanted us to be dedicated to God's will and purpose.

Dedication to an unseen God, who rewards us in private, is outside our realm of experience. That makes it difficult for us to concentrate on spiritual activity. Yet this is the very activity that lets us "see" our invisible God.

Purity is to be free from taint or pollution. It is to have unmixed desires. In this verse, it does not mean you must be sinless before you can see God. You must simply want to be pure in thought, word, and deed. When you want to "clean up your act," you have made a start on this beatitude. You will become pure in the full sense only after God himself removes your impure thoughts and acts. God purifies you.

Here Jesus teaches that your heart-your thoughts, feelings and emotions—must concentrate on meeting God. Knowing and pleasing God needs to be so important to you that it is your main desire. When you make this your priority, God will come to you. He will reveal Himself to you so dramatically it is as if you have actually seen Him.

Your face-to-face encounter with God proves His reality and nature. "Seeing" God, and knowing Him as Abba—your Daddy— is the blessing promised in this beatitude.

NOTES

PEACE ···

"Blessed are the peacemakers: for they shall be called the children of God" (Matt. 5:9). This sounds simple enough. Peacemakers are called God's children. By whom? When? Why? Where? Will this buy bread?

Most people think peace is a good idea, as long as they get their way. When they don't get their way, there is hell to pay. Even the Soviets talked peace—"mir"—while they were the world's leading terrorists, planning world conquest.

Peace, according to Jesus, starts within personal attitudes and behavior. In the "Sermon," Jesus detailed this project. We are told not to return evil with evil. We are to turn the other cheek, do what is asked of us, and forgive affronts. We are to love unconditionally, always treating others as we would want to be treated if our roles were reversed. We are to forget ourselves, never retaliate, and let hostilities stop with us.

Sounds impossible, doesn't it? It is, except for God's promise that you will be blessed and will be called—known as—children of God. What He asks you to do, He will empower you to accomplish. His grace is sufficient.

What does it mean to be called God's child? What would it mean to you if your father was President of the United States, or king of a great nation, or some famous celebrity? You would be famous by association, privileged in many ways, and protected by his position.

So it is when you are a child of God. God oversees your life, handles your retaliations in His own way, and protects your person. He continually sends you blessings, both spiritual and material. You get what you want and need by His grace. Peacemaking brings peace and harmony into your life.

NOTES

PERSECUTION ·······························

Along with the good news comes some bad news. There had to be a catch somewhere, didn't there? Well, here it is in both the eighth and ninth beatitudes. Blessings and rewards are still there, but persecutions are added. *"Blessed are they which are persecuted for righteousness sake, for theirs is the kingdom of heaven"* (Matt. 5:10). Persecutions? Who wants them?

In the fourth beatitude, Jesus asked you to hunger and thirst after righteousness. Now He says you could be persecuted if you are righteous. But He says don't worry about it. You will be blessed with the benefits of the Kingdom of Heaven.

Let's discuss persecution and also the Kingdom of Heaven. The standard definition of persecuted means to be harassed. Types and degrees of harassment can vary. The fact is that some will seek to injure you in one way or the other because you are righteous. They know they reflect poorly in your new light.

When you turn from worldliness and all that means, and seek a face-to-face relationship with God, you change. Your outlook and goals become spiritual instead of material. Now you are different. This threatens those who don't understand that life's base is spiritual.

In the natural, people put goods first and God second. Now you have put God first and goods second. Your outlook seems to be crazy. You are crazy, but you are crazy like the fox. You now have the best of this life and the life yet to come.

You know that when God takes control of your life, He makes good things happen. Those blessings happen because of His love and grace, not because of conniving or striving. When God is in control, goods follow grace as gifts. This is the Kingdom of Heaven.

NOTES

JESUS ···

In history, Jesus has received mixed reviews. Ideas about Him are called *Christology* and no summary of them is needed here. Many of those ideas are simply folk lore with no factual basis. One thing we do know for sure about Jesus: He said you will have trouble because of Him. How can that happen to you? What association will you have with Jesus that can cause you problems? What will you two be doing?

The ninth beatitude records, *"Blessed are you, when men shall revile you, and persecute you, and shall say all manner of evil against you falsely, for my sake. Rejoice, and be exceedingly glad: for great is your reward in heaven: for so persecuted they the prophets which were before you"* (Matt. 5:11-12).

So you are going to be reviled? You? Yes, you are going to be "bad mouthed"—taunted, upbraided, chided, grieved, harassed, and criticized. For Jesus' sake! Are you ready for this? Probably not, but ready or not, if you take Jesus seriously and report Him favorably, you are in for that.

Why is this? It is because He is grossly misunderstood by the masses. They think Jesus came to shut down their party and turn out the lights. The masses have no idea that Jesus came to start a *real* party, the biggest party the world has ever known, with lights so bright they light up the world.

But, if you take him seriously and stick to this course, when you graduate, He will give you a party. There is something great in store for you. Great is your coming reward. You are soon to be blessed beyond measure. Did you notice Jesus compares you to the prophets of old? What does He mean?

He means this. When you meet Jesus, and realize what He really did for you, you will become his energetic supporter. You will be telling about Jesus and God's mighty works. People who don't like Jesus won't like you. Remember the feeling?

NOTES

CONFUSION ·······································

We hunger to know the truth about all things, especially the nature of life. This search for life's meaning is a part of every age and every culture.

It is only natural that great thinkers of each society have searched for explanations of existence. Often those thinkers come to believe they have found the truth, or most of it, of "what life is all about." Each promoted his opinions as "Truth" and became revered as a great and wise teacher. A few of those thinkers have their opinions remembered as "Great Religions" that are still followed in our time.

Conflicts and competition between these religions cause much confusion. Many doubt that any universally accepted truth can be distilled out of the conflict. So, we are challenged to pick the "right" religion and to justify our choice.

"Why," some ask, "shouldn't everyone be skeptical about religious opinion and which one is correct? Who can know what to believe when there are so many different opinions?"

Going further, they challenge with, "You have cited Jesus as your religious authority. Why choose Jesus instead of Moses, Mohammed, Krishna, Buddha, Confucius, or Zoroaster?"

We must start with Jesus because His beliefs have most influenced Western civilization. This is where we live and where we are constantly confronted with Jesus' name, example, and ideas. Because of that, His words and works are most familiar and easiest to find for study. Let's begin to test what we know about Jesus to see what we can prove or disprove.

72

NOTES

CHALLENGE ··

There are two particularly telling claims about Jesus wherein each person can test Him and personally know the results. The problem with the two tests is that they cannot be used simply as spiritual parlor games. Jesus confirms His truths only to those who sincerely want a continuing face-to-face relationship with God.

One of Jesus' earliest comments is that, *"You shall not tempt the Lord God"* (Matt. 4:7). By that He meant, God will not allow you to paint Him into a corner. You cannot put God into a position that requires His response. If you could, God would be in your control, always subject to your manipulation. He would only be an actor in a spiritual dog-and-pony show.

Sincerity is one prerequisite for God's response. When we honestly want a dependency relationship with God, we get it. The dependency God requires is different from the dependency we always preferred. God wants His children dependent on Him. As selfish people, we wanted God to be dependent on us. We thought He should do what we wanted instead of the other way around. Once we understand His priorities, and know we must be subject to Him, He shows up when asked.

With that understanding, you can depend on God proving that Jesus was resurrected. Next, you can depend on God to send the baptism of the Holy Spirit as Jesus promised.

Jesus said He had to "go away" before He could send the Holy Spirit but the Spirit would come and be with you forever. He also promised He would not leave you desolate and that He would come for you (John 14:15-20; 16:7-11). If these promises are kept, Jesus is proved. If they are not kept, Jesus is disproved. Now let's ask Jesus to fulfill these promises.

NOTES

REBIRTH ···

Jesus made a requirement for the complete spiritual life. He said, *"Verily, verily, I say unto thee, Except a man be born again, he cannot see the kingdom of God"* (John 3:3). A fuller explanation follows in verses five through eight.

"Verily, verily, I say unto thee, Except a man be born of water and of the Spirit, he cannot enter into the Kingdom of God. That which is born of flesh is flesh; and that which is born of Spirit is spirit. Marvel not that I said unto thee, Ye must be born again. The wind bloweth where it listeth, and thou hearest the sound thereof, but canst not tell whence it cometh, and whither it goeth: so is everyone who is born of the Spirit" (John 3:5-8).

Being born of the Spirit requires an act of God. Only Jesus can give you the rebirth that allows you to enter into the Kingdom of God. This act of grace separates Jesus from other teachers and pretenders. Ask Jesus for the rebirth and you will receive it. His ability to do this confirms His nature.

If you seriously want a full time working partnership with the God of creation, tell Him. The traditional prayer for your rebirth (at-one-ness with God) includes repentance, confession, and a petition for forgiveness and the rebirth. Say this prayer twice to be sure the words are truly yours.

Jesus, I want to be born again. I want this grace and the spiritual Kingdom of Heaven you promised. Please forgive my past and put your spirit into my heart. If you are truly the Savior of the World and the Son of God, I want you to be my Lord and leader. Now, take over my life, let me be born again. Use me as you choose.

NOTES

POWER ·······································

The second promise from Jesus that we need to test is His promise to send the Holy Spirit to live in us forever. If that commitment is not fulfilled, all other claims for Jesus fall to the ground. John, in the fourth Gospel, records this promise and the nature of the Holy Spirit (John 16:7-16).

There are at least thirty-four direct references to the Holy Spirit in the New Testament (Appendix B). The Holy Spirit is the essence of God that comes to live in each person who wants to be His *temple*, the temple of the Holy Spirit.

Receiving this portion of God's power and presence in us is known as being baptized with the Holy Spirit (Acts 1:5-8). There Jesus promised the Holy Spirit would come and bring God's power into His followers. That unusual event occurred as He promised on the Day of Pentecost (Acts 2).

The Holy Spirit teaches us, comforts us, guides us, and gives us the power to be children of God (subjects of His Kingdom) while still living in this world. Also, the Holy Spirit changes our outlook on life and keeps us from returning to worldly wants and selfishness.

Once we receive this portion of God's essence, His reality and primacy become our guiding principle. We know, without any doubt, that existence is spiritual, eternal, and in God's hands. Our only desire and duty is to know and cooperate with God's mind and will. Now is the time to ask Jesus for the baptism with the Holy Spirit and power (*fire*).

NOTES

FIRE ··

John the Baptist prophesied that Jesus would baptize with the Holy Spirit and fire (Matt. 3:11-12, Mark 1:7-8, Luke 3:15-17). Jesus said He had to *go away* before the Holy Spirit could be sent (John 16:7).

Later, after His death, Jesus told His followers to wait in Jerusalem and they would receive the Holy Spirit and power (Acts 1:4-8). They waited. On the Day of Pentecost, all were amazed when the Holy Spirit fell on each person in the group, with visible *tongues of fire* as confirmation (Acts 2:1-21, especially verses 3 and 4). Christianity's validity and vitality depend on God baptizing all who seek this gift.

Two important things happen to every person who receives this spiritual experience. First, baptism with the Holy Spirit witnesses to the truth of Jesus (John 15:26,27). Jesus' promises about the Holy Spirit are fulfilled for you. Next, when God's power overcomes you, you are changed. Now you can witness to the reality of God from your personal experience.

Read these New Testament citations. If you believe them, you will become willing to receive the baptism with the Spirit. As you asked to be reborn in the prior section, ask God to baptize you with the Holy Spirit. Jesus said all you have to do is ask (Luke 11:9-13).

The Holy Spirit proceeds from God the Father and Jesus, God's son (John 14:12-17), so a prayer to the Father in Jesus' name is appropriate. When you seriously want this spiritual experience, ask and keep asking until you receive it (Luke 11:5-13; 18:1-8).

NOTES

FRUIT ···

When we read the Beatitudes, the attitudes Jesus requires are good ideas but appear to be mainly unattainable. We would always like to be merciful, mild, peacemakers who seek righteous behavior. Beatitude attitudes are described more easily than they are effected.

After receiving the baptism with the Holy Spirit, we are different. We have been changed and have power to be what God always intended us to be. So, God begins to grow fruit of the Spirit in our lives. The Apostle Paul described this in his letter to the Galatians (5:22-24). He said the fruits of the spirit are love, joy, peace, patience, kindness, goodness, faithfulness, gentleness, and self-control.

In the past, we were captive to worldly ideas and behavior that Paul called *works of the flesh*. Reviewing his list brings on some bad memories to many of us. We wonder about our past behavior. Adultery, fornication, uncleanness, idolatry, witchcraft, hatred, strife, anger, lying, envy, jealousy, dissension, drunkenness, unclean thoughts, and carousing are some of the problems we have when we live apart from God (Gal. 5:19-21).

When living the new life in the Spirit, we grow out of the works of the flesh as we grow into the fruit of the Spirit. This change brings new contentment and thanksgiving for it.

We are so different, we wonder how this could happen. Others also recognize we are a new person in *Christ*. Some like us and some don't, but we like our new self. It is as if a load of bricks has been lifted from our back. We are free from a life that we couldn't control or change. The chains that limited us are cut and we can be the person we always knew we were destined to be.

NOTES

GIFTS ···

On page seventy-seven, you read about the Holy Spirit giving power. The most important gift of power is your power to be a new spiritual person. You, as a new person, are now mainly concerned with pleasing God. You best do this by receiving, experiencing and living in the fruit of the Spirit: love, joy, peace, patience, kindness, goodness, faithfulness, gentleness, and self-control.

To equip us to do this, the Holy Spirit offers power tools. These are what Paul calls gifts (charismata) of the Spirit, to be used for the common good—for the benefit of all in God's family. Once you receive the Holy Spirit, by asking for it, you are in God's family. You can expect to be given one or more spiritual gifts. Paul listed these in his first letter to the Corinthians, chapter twelve, verses four through thirteen.

The gifts are wisdom, knowledge, faith, healing, miracles, prophecy, discernment of spirits, speaking in tongues, and interpretation of tongues. Power gifts are given as God chooses, when God chooses, to implement God's work on earth.

These gifts come and go, ebb and flow, according to God's will. No one has the same gift at all times to be used by some formula or mechanical fashion.

What is demonstrated in supernatural gifts is God's special grace as distinguished from His *general* (prevenient) grace. God is always in control of creation. He is everywhere, knows all things, and is all powerful. His general grace, necessary for life on earth, is experienced by everyone—"*for he makes his sun to rise on the evil and the good, and sends rain on the just and the unjust*" (Matt. 5:45 b).

His *special* grace is given to improve human faith. These gifts demonstrate His reality and omnipotence. Charismatic gifts are for giving glory to God. Any who use this special grace for self-glory have a future problem to work out with God (Matt. 7:21-23). It is a good idea to keep out of that kind of mess by waiting for God's direction. Give him all the credit for any supernatural gifts you receive.

NOTES

DOCTRINE ....

The faith that Jesus brought to earth is distinct from any other religion. It is a religion of the heart. It is based on what you receive, not what you believe. The presence and power of God in your life come because of who you know and not because of what you know. There are no works—rituals and liturgies—that brought God to you and into your heart. He came be cause you wanted Him there. The transaction was based totally on a common agreement between you and God.

It is wonderful that you don't have to "buy" God's grace by what you do or do not do—good, bad, or indifferent. You simply asked God to take over your life and he agreed to do so. He didn't ask about your race, sex, age, education, religious ideas, or past life. All He asked was for your permission to come into your life and be your God. You accepted His request. He came in, and you were born again. Now you love Him because He first loved you (1 John 4:19).

This is why Jesus' religion is the one true religion. For the first and only time in world history, He taught about, and opened a way to God that is available to everyone. It is effective for everyone, therefore it is a universal faith. No other religion has this simple door to God. None understand it. All organized religions insist you must do certain acts (works) to get into the divine door and stay in God's favor.

You met God face-to-face by His gift of free grace, only because you wanted to meet Him. You asked Him to come to you and run your life. You may be tempted to review His gift and imagine that some particular thought you had, or act you did, caused God's grace to fall on you. To add on any condition beyond simply asking is called heresy. "Add-ons" are invented doctrines— side roads—that are spiritual traps. Add-ons can separate you from God and dry up your childlike blind trust. Add-ons deny God's free grace. In the past, disputes over worthless add-ons have caused religious persecutions and wars. In our time, they stress and divide people of faith. Avoid them to keep your blind trust and childlike faith.

NOTES

BIBLE ....

When you get serious about God, you want to start your own research. Having a dynamic spiritual experience quickly makes you realize you want to learn all you can about what happened to you. In the western world the Judeo-Christian tradition prevails. So you naturally turn to the Bible, its holy book, as the accepted depository of God information.

You wonder, "Where should I start? What does the Bible mean? Why two Testaments, an old one and a new one?" Bible means books and comes from the Greek word *biblia*. The Bible is the primary history of God's actions and revelations as recorded by Jews and early Christians.

It covers the period from creation (Adam) through Jesus' last disciple (John) who died at the end of the first century A.D. Its two-part division is for two epochs of human history. Old is before Jesus (BC) and the new epoch is after Jesus' birth, Anno Domini (AD). Testament simply means testimony about, or witness to those two historical epochs.

For Jews and Judaism, only the Old Testament is sacred—most especially, the record from Abraham (c. 1800 BC) through Malachi (c.460 BC). Judaism is rooted in the first five Old Testament books, known as the Law (Torah), or the books of Moses. The Old Testament divides into the Law, the Prophets, and the Writings. It records a history of a closed religious era, and how God once worked exclusively with tribal Jews through their temple and monarchy.

For Christians and Christianity, the New Testament is the place to start. Both Testaments are sacred but the New Testament records Jesus' new epoch, the start of the Kingdom of God on Earth. We live in the New Covenant era. Jesus closed the "Old" epoch. Jesus' death on the cross changed everything and brought in His New Covenant. Jesus made God easily available. He is freely open to all people who want to be in His presence.

NOTES

ORDER ....

God is a master planner and the architect of order. Examine this statement for yourself. Have you ever seen the sun rise in the west and set in the east? Do you know of any event where down was up and up was down? Is not water always wet and dust always dry? Summers are warm and winters are cool.

Predictable order is the foundation for our survival. You were born as a child, not as an adult, and developed at a predictable rate. When you began your education, you were ignorant. You finished educated. Part of your education was learning how to read a book. You were taught all books start at their first page and end at their last word. To properly read a book, you read it in that order—from front to back.

This is because the writer, or author, is presenting a theme you will miss if you do not follow his order. The New Testament is a book, supplied to you in order. It exists by divine inspiration, directed by the Holy Spirit. Simply said, God put His hand on the New Testament and its order. Read it in His order to learn His rules and purpose for you.

Because faith is for everyone, regardless of age, education, intelligence or culture, God must be easily understood. That is true for God's book. It is easy to understand when its order is followed. The Holy Spirit gives you the understanding.

Pick a translation that suits you. Start at Matthew 1:1 and slowly work toward its end at Revelation 22:21. You will not understand it all. Pass over ancient, mysterious customs that frame its stories. Think about meanings of the events. Meanings will emerge for you. You will understand all you need as you go along, and more as you continue to meditate. Bible reading is not to turn you into a Bible expert. That takes a lifetime of study. Reading it lets God speak to you through it. Bible reading helps Him develop you into the person He planned you to be from time's beginning. As you read and meditate, God changes your thoughts and behavior.

90

NOTES

WORKS ··

The good news about a life of faith in God's kingdom is that He is in control. Along with His authority over you, He continues to have responsibility for you. It is as if He says to you, "The buck stops here." God is working for your well being.

When you took Jesus' teachings seriously, and accepted them for your way of life, you won God's protection. From then on you became God's responsibility. He is your protector. You know this from the "Lord's Prayer." God is your *Abba*, Daddy. You do not need to do more religious works to prod Him.

Rituals, liturgies, prayer formulas, piety, or special knowledge are not needed. He is working in your life because He loves you, and not because of what you do. All your Father wants from you is acknowledgment that He is the source of your good fortune. He appreciates your gratitude.

Living in God's Kingdom of Heaven is that simple. All you say is, "God is God, and I am His child, and He is taking care of me. I will do my best and He will make all things work out for good." For some people, that is too simple.

Faith is accepting life as it is, without complaint. It is knowing God will work out all things for your benefit, sooner or later. Lack of faith is losing trust in God's willingness to protect you and pour His love and providence into your life. God never forgets a name. He will never leave you or forsake you. Your name is engraved in His mind.

When things are not going according to *your* plans, you can become frustrated. Things are not supposed to work out according to your plans. Don't forget, you turned yourself over to Him some time ago. Final planning is in His hands, not yours. No amount of religious works can change that.

NOTES

GRACE ··

A most interesting commonality found in all cultures is the belief that some act, or work, will best please God. Thus, every culture has folklore about rituals and liturgies they believe can influence the mind of the creator. Rites and chants, to control events or move God, are magic. They are only superstitions with no Biblical basis.

Think about this moment. If someone can invent a way to get God to do whatever is desired, who is God? If a person can move God on command by acts, so they directly control God, then God has become man's instrument. Who wants a God that can be directed by someone you don't even know? Scary!

God is even-handed and just. He acts only with fairness. He loves you so much, He will never put anyone's interests ahead of yours. Sometimes it seems as if you are being ignored but you are not. Usually it just takes God a little time to bring your wants into fruition. His grace never leaves you.

Further, what you think you want, by your limited vision and experience, may not be the same as your deepest "heart's desire." You want the fruit of the Spirit in your life. You do not want anything that can detract from that ultimate heart's desire. Short-sighted wants may really be a cursing that can only be understood in hindsight. God will not give you anything that will damage you. You really want a life blessed with the fruit of the Spirit and the presence of God. Worldly pleasures can be hindrances to your receiving those blessings. Instant pleasures can become curses later.

So we ask for God's grace and blessings on our life. We know He knows what we need and want before we even ask. With His love and wisdom, He plans better for us than we can plan for ourselves. We have no need to manipulate Him by works. We now know His love and grace is free. Simple asking is the only Biblical formula for obtaining grace. God's office is always open, so we can call on Him anytime. His ears are strong and His memory never fails. *"Ask and ye will receive"* (Matt. 7:7).

94

NOTES

LIFE ···

It is certain that you and I exist. I know I do, and you know you do. Why there is life, instead of no life, we do not know. Although we do not have an answer to that great mystery, we know there are two dimensions to life, material and spiritual. We live in the material but we are affected by the spiritual. Your meeting with God proved that.

Somewhere along mankind's way into this century, people have downgraded or denied the spiritual facet of life. Most are rationalists who believe only what can be physically proved. Ancient traditions about spiritual powers and presences in this world are ridiculed and forgotten.

Ideas of an ever present theistic God have been mocked. Our concern about God's reality has melted under the pressure of jokes and derision. Called everything from superstition to lunacy, interest in living with daily trust and faith in God has almost disappeared. Showing faith in public is embarrassing.

Cynicism about God has caused a denial of any evil spiritual dimension of life. Acknowledgment of the devil (Satan) and evil spirits (demons) is gone from sophisticated conversation. Ideas about Satan being the author of evil and sin are considered to be the exclusive property of the ignorant. Spiritual understandings of evil and the spiritual realm have almost ended.

In recent years, a little news about Satanism and Satanic Cults has emerged. Lacking background information, few are willing and able to investigate Satanism. Too many still remember the tragically foolish Salem witch hunts.

A quick walk through the New Testament shows Jesus' contest with Satan and demons is a strong and continuing theme. Paul specifically taught our battle is with the spirit world (Eph. 6:12). We need to understand this warfare and how we can win it. This is the action side of our life in faith.

NOTES

SATAN ··

God's protection and providence should be enough for any-one, but there is even more. Another part of being in the Kingdom of Heaven is the action part. God lets you do His work on earth, using Jesus' delegated power and authority.

A special way we share Jesus' power is by casting out demons in His name, by His authority. In early Christianity, even children cast out demons. You can also, and should. To run this experiment, you need to know what a bad spirit is, what they do, and where they reside. Look at your own experience.

Satan's program is to make you miserable. He wants to disrupt your personal relationships and keep you from enjoying the fruit of the Spirit. He sends bad spirits to harass and vex you with unhap-py moods and dangerous mental attitudes. That causes you to think and act (sin) in ways that keep you from enjoying the fruit of the Spirit.

His immediate goal is to cause conflicts and to ravage your self-image. He attacks your sense of accomplishment and the value of it. His ultimate goal is to make you so unhappy you wish you were dead. He wants you to consider suicide.

Fortunately, bad spirits must disclose who they are. They always tell you their names. When you confess any negative feeling, it is a spirit giving its name. So, if you say, "I am depressed," the spirit of Depression is naming itself.

This rule applies to all your unholy feelings. When you say you have envy, lust, anger, resentment, fear, despair, pride, depression, greed, rage, sloth, lying, strife, licentious, doubt, anxiety, or any other negative, a spirit is saying its own name. Knowing its name is the start for casting it out.

NOTES

LORD ···

Casting out demons, as well as all other positive spiritual duties, is done with power delegated from Jesus. Binding and casting out demons is always done "in Jesus' name." The name of Jesus is not a magic word. His name is a literary code that represents His person, just as your name defines and describes your personality.

Praying in Jesus' name is asking God to act because "Jesus" in Hebrew means "God saves," or "God save us." Praying the name "Jesus" is also a statement of faith. Jesus' name declares He is God —"Lord"—God's face in an earthly presence.

When Jesus left this life, He promised to send you the Holy Spirit and power. You receive that "baptism with fire" by asking for it. The power you received, delegated from Jesus, is to be used to continue His work on earth. You must use the power you have received, especially for binding and casting out bad spirits— demons. Mark 16:14-17 lists some of your duties and the authority Jesus gave you. You studied Paul's list of powers on the page named "Gifts."

To cast out spirits, *repentance* and *confession* are needed. The word repentance simply means you want to be rid of bad feelings and acts. Some people want to hold on to bad feelings. So, they might confess they have anger, but want to harbor it. You can keep a bad feeling if you want to stay unhappy. Anytime you want to be rid of it, repent, or regret you have the unhappy feeling. Once you repent and confess a bad spirit, casting it out is easy. It has to go when you tell it to go.

Simply say, "Spirit of (name), I bind you in Jesus' name. I cast you out in Jesus' name. By His authority, you must go. Go now, quickly and quietly." Your attitude will change immediately.

If the spirit rebels or becomes hostile, just be firm. Occasionally, demons try to test your faith. You have *full* authority and it must go. It has no options. Continue commanding it to leave in Jesus' name and it will. No loud talk is needed, only your firmness and resolve.

NOTES

WOUNDS ···

You know yourself fairly well, almost as completely as God knows you. It is difficult to keep secrets from Him, so you might as well get that old stuff out in the open. That *old stuff* is your entire past. It includes all the mistakes you have made, as well as all the bad things others did to you.

Every mistake you regret was done from ignorance. If you could have, you would have done better. How often have you said, "I am doing the best I can." That is a true statement. You do your best, but often your best is not good enough.

If you want that consideration, you must give it to others. Everyone is doing the best they can at the time they carry out their act. The problem is our best act is too often not good enough. Bad consequences can occur from wrong acts. Wrong acts come from bad emotions and incomplete information. We get wronged as we wrong others, because all are imperfect.

Having good intent to do your best does not free you from consequences. What you have wrongly done can make you feel guilty and ashamed. What has been done wrongly to you also leaves you with emotional wounds. There can be very strong emotional reactions to life's events. All emotions affect choices long after an event's immediate significance.

The simplest way to say this is all that has happened to you affects your emotions and will govern your actions. If you have unhappy feelings and behave in irrational ways, it is because of your past experiences. Those bad feelings, the bad spirits and the demons, live in unhealed emotional wounds. Until God heals that wound, it will continue to produce bad spirits.

Emotional wounds are similar to physical wounds. Untreated they become infected and stay infected. Emotional pain and damaged behavior results. Have the demons you sent away crept back in? If so, it is because the emotional wound where they live is not healed. It is time to have permanent healing of bad memories and their damage repaired.

102

NOTES

HEALING ··

One of the most overlooked, or often ignored, teaching of Jesus is Matthew 6:6-8. There He says, *"But when you pray, go into your room and shut the door and pray to your Father who is in secret; and your Father who is in secret will reward you. And in praying do not heap up empty phrases as the Gentiles do; for they think they will be heard for their many words. Do not be like them, for your Father knows what you need before you ask him."*

Most of us think prayer is a matter of telling God what we want, and then waiting for Him to deliver. The idea of being quiet and waiting for God to act fades from lack of faith. When you are still, Jesus will come to you. Invite Him in.

In the "Lord's Prayer" you read about God's will. Let God's will be done now. Be still, with eyes closed, and wait for the Lord. Ask Jesus to bring into your mind a scene or event that needs healing. Be patient and soon a memory will appear in your "mind's eye." Ask Jesus to come into the scene and "look around" for Him. You will know when He is there. You will either "see" Him or feel His presence. Watch what He does. He will minister to you in a personal way, so dynamic you know the experience is real. You will be changed.

Each time a scene ends with His healing action, ask Him for another. When no more come, ask Him if He wants you to stop or wait for another scene. He will let you know. When you are sure His visit has ended, thank Him for coming.

If possible, have another person of faith with you when you ask for this healing. Spiritual events can be more dynamic when two or more pray together. To understand this, look at Matthew 18:19-20 and James 5:16.

NOTES

VARIETY ···

There is a famous old expression that "variety is the spice of life." Imagine what life would be like if there were no variety. Everyone would look the same. There would be only one color, a single smell, and only one musical note. All would cook the same recipes, paint the same pictures, and write the same books. How could we ever tell each other apart? It wouldn't matter what house we went to at night or what job we did each day. We couldn't know and sort out our own children and all would have the same type of pet.

God put variety in creation to spare us that impossible mess. No two things will ever be alike. Even clones will not be alike because their histories are different. Their different environments keep them from thinking alike. They cannot act the same, even if physically identical. God's law of variety keeps life exciting and that law is irrevocable.

Why bother to discuss anything that is so obvious? We must, because there is a personality characteristic in people that always objects to the law of variety. Everyone has that particular trait. We want our opinions to be the commonly agreed standards. We believe everyone should agree with us. We dispute with any who disagree. Our disagreements cause hot arguments and broken relationships. How strange! We adore variety yet we deplore differences. Our variety causes strife. Those two are together forever.

Many well-intentioned people believe conformity of religious ideas and practices is God's absolute will. Some will try to proselytize you into a particular denominational system, and insist it is God's one true church. You might say, "If your church is superior, your members should be better than other people and more pleasing to God. Are they? How so?"

Jesus taught us to judge a tree by its fruit. Good trees have good fruit. Good theology produces good religion that produces the fruit of the Spirit. Check for fruit. See the list on page eighty-one. Review page ninety-one on Works and especially remember it's paragraph three.

NOTES

TEACHERS ··

We humans have inquiring minds that enjoy exploring life's events. We have automatic computers in our heads that make us search every incident to find a better way to do whatever we just did. Our self-preservation instinct drives us to find ways to make life happier, simpler, better, and stress-less. We hate problems, love ease, and revere anyone who offers to teach us an easier, better way to live.

Our search for better ways requires us to seek sage teachers and listen to their wisdom. All convincing teachers gather followers. The more attractive the teacher, the larger is their following. Charismatic personalties can capture the minds of whole nations. This phenomena requires attention.

The information we automatically seek must come from a teacher. We trust our teachers to deliver truths. Usually we receive our teacher's offerings without any critique. In school, our scores depended on that. We accepted what the teacher transmitted, because we had no way to measure the accuracy of new and unfamiliar subject matter. We were defenseless against false teaching. What protection can we have that will automatically filter out wrong information?

There is a defense. Learn the difference between fact and opinion. Responsibly separate the two. Always remember, most every thing you hear is simply opinion. Your discretion is absolutely vital on spiritual matters. The only spiritual *fact* is actual Scripture as it was originally written in the languages of Hebrew and Greek. Commentaries are not fact and Bible translations are only opinions about original meanings.

Anything taught about Bible texts beyond exact original language readings, is commentary and only opinion. It is unfortunate that most spiritual teachers present their opinions as fact, failing to distinguish between the two. Many do not separate the two covenants. Mixing scriptures from both New and Old Covenants confuses even more. Test everything carefully. Prove all things for yourself. Never accept, teach, or imply opinion and hearsay as final truth.

NOTES

CHURCH ···

All cults have a common characteristic. Each starts with one person who believes he or she has a new and unique revelation about life that no one else has. Speaking as a "teacher" of mysteries, this teacher authoritatively claims these new ideas are the only "correct" way to associate with God. Once some like-minded people collect together as followers, these "true" believers announce they are the "true" church. Anyone who thinks contrary, and disagrees, is shunned. Shunning goes beyond clannishness and may lead to hostility. Violence, murder, and martyrdom have resulted. Cultic thinking and behavior has been man's lot from time's beginning.

So, we see that a cult is a group of people who insist their unique beliefs are essential for relationship with God. They join together, manufacture a holy book, acquiesce to their leader, proselytize new members, shun all who disagree, and comfort themselves by imagining they are superior. Cults are aggressive and hard to avoid. They seldom hide.

Jesus' church is entirely different. It is spiritual, not physical. Membership is through a connection to God and not through strange ideas. You made your connection when you met God and felt Him in your "heart." All who are spiritually connected with God in this same manner are members of Jesus' church. His church is the "ekklesia," simply God's community of believers. Our leader is God the Father as revealed by Jesus. All who are at one with God by faith are in the Kingdom of God, the ekklesia, now and for eternity.

Our oneness with God because of Jesus is the major theme of the New Testament. Jesus taught we are all children of our heavenly Father. Our equality before God is described in Paul's letter to the Galatians. He wrote, *"There is neither Jew nor Greek, there is neither slave nor free, there is neither male nor female; for you are all one in Christ Jesus,"* (Gal. 3:28). Understanding our unity with God helps us understand our unity with each other. When we are at one with God, we cooperate in unity. Competition and exclusiveness is outside God's will for us. Unconditional (agape) love for God and our fellow is God's law for us. Cults limit their love to those who subscribe to their demands.

NOTES

IMAGE ·····························

The well known story of Adam's creation declares that man was made in the image of God. We know now mankind is anything but in the image of God. We discussed man's inhumanity to man on page twenty-five. Jesus' work both on earth and in Heaven, is to show us what is the image of God and to make the way for miraculously restoring us to it.

When you received the rebirth and were baptized with the Holy Spirit, you were restored to the image of God. Your nature became the same as Jesus. We say Jesus is "fully human and fully divine." You are also. You are a human who is also the temple of the Holy Spirit. You have received the same God Spirit that Jesus received, (1 Cor. 3:16,17; 6:19).

You have a different life to live and job to do than Jesus, but you are in the same image and have His same spiritual powers (resources). If you and He were not alike, He would not be a realistic example. We are different from Jesus only in duties and personal histories. He was sinless from birth. You and I were sinners from birth. He knew God's will from birth, but we are just beginning to understand and seek His will.

Jesus put so much emphasis on being in God's will, and doing God's will, we expect Him to show us a simple formula to help us do it. We want a clear step-by-step program so we can be sure we are always in God's will. Jesus showed us a simple way but endless added rituals and liturgies have muddled it.

Jesus taught a right mental attitude is required to get into God's will. You learned that attitude at the first beatitude. You must want to be in His will. God blesses your desire. The "system" is to sincerely give God your life and will to do with you as He pleases. There is a first time for this, and also daily repetition. This is known as taking up your cross daily to follow Jesus. Surrender of self to God is an attitude of trust and humility. Simply ask and expect God to direct, correct, and protect you.

NOTES

TRUST ·····································

All American money reminds us, "In God We Trust." By now, you know that trusting God is much easier said than done, and much more than repeating a national slogan. You learned trusting God is not a matter of words. It is a matter of the heart. Trust in God grows out of life's experiences.

First you hear about faith, then you try it. Good results prove God is real. As you trust Him more, your faith grows. Each time you see His blessings, you trust Him more.

There are at least four degrees of trusting God. At the start of your spiritual walk, you neither know God nor trust Him. Trust is only a question. Can you trust God? If so, when, why, and how? This is, "In God We Trust?"

Next is "In God We Trust;" (followed with a semi-colon). At this stage you trust little, and add works to gain God's attention. God is offered trades, rituals, prayers, and repeated liturgies. It is as if to say, "God, see what I am doing for you? Don't I rate a favor?" This is not trusting God. It is trusting your "add-ons," hoping to gain God's favor with bribes.

Then there is "In God We Trust." A period ends the statement when you find yourself without a solution to an ominous situation. Sometimes life paints you into corners that leave no choices and have no options. There is no time to bribe and nothing to do but grit your teeth and say, "God help me, I have no place to go." This is called "fox hole religion." When your ordeal is over, you act as if it were a one-time event. It is easy to forget free trust worked. You quickly return to "add ons." The semi-colon comes back to replace the period.

After a few of these fox hole experiences, you learn God is real. You say by faith, "In God We Trust! Yahoo! Isn't God wonderful? He looks after me all the time." He does the work, and you are the beneficiary. Your wait and your long walk were worth it. You trust God completely. He is your Father, your *Abba*, your Daddy. God's endless grace abounds. In God we trust!

NOTES

APPENDIX A / COUNSELOR ·····························

Moving from a lifetime of little or no faith into a face to face encounter with God can be intimidating. More than that, it can be an embarrassing experience. Many are reluctant to even start this adventure. God understands.

God has both a sense of humor and plenty of patience. He is also honest and keeps His promises. He maintains His true nature. God is omnipresent, is everywhere, and has always been with you. So, believe it or not, He knows your every thought and act. You really don't need to tell Him much about yourself.

He will be happy to assist you to understand the pages of this book. Just ask Him to give you understanding. Tell Him you do not want to be misled and you want to know the truth and nothing but the truth.

If you lack practice in prayer, you might start with the famous doubter's prayer, " Oh God, if there is a God, help me if you can."

Many people have started here. They simply prayed seriously for the first time. Ask only for guidance and understanding. This will give God an opportunity to show Himself to you and start you on a path of dynamic, powerful faith.

"Hello, God. Are you out there? Let me hear from you. I want to meet you face to face."

NOTES

APPENDIX B / HOLY SPIRIT ·······························

Jesus promised to send the Holy Spirit after leaving earth. Events on the day of Pentecost, and continually since, prove the promise was kept. Without this actual confirmation of Jesus' promise, He would drop out of history as another false prophet. This promise is on the list below at item 11. Its first fulfillment on Pentecost is at item 18. Following is a list of New Testament scripture about the Holy Spirit.

1. Matthew 3:11,12; Mark 1:7,8; Luke 3:15-17. John the Baptist announces Jesus' ministry and purpose.
2. Matthew 3:13-17; Mark 1:9-11; Luke 3:21-23. Jesus' baptism with water was unnecessary. He did it to "fulfill all righteousness" and visibly received the Holy Spirit.
3. Luke 1:26-38 (esp. 34,35). Jesus fathered by the Holy Spirit, and of the Holy Spirit, but baptized with the Holy Spirit after John's baptism.
4. Matthew 4:1; Mark 1:12; Luke 4:1. Jesus led by Holy Spirit.
5. John 1:19-34 (esp. 32-34). John the Baptist affirms Jesus' baptism with the Holy Spirit.
6. John 2:23-3:15 (esp. 3:1-9). Jesus teaches a spiritual rebirth is necessary.
7. John 3:22-36 (esp. 34,35). John affirms that Jesus had the Holy Spirit without measure.
8. Luke 12:10. Disbelief of the Holy Spirit is sin.
9. Luke 12:11,12. The Holy Spirit is our teacher who removes anxiety.
10. John 7:37-39, 14:15-17. Jesus promises the Holy Spirit, "living water" from His heart, "the Spirit of Truth."
11. John 14:18-31 (esp. 23,25,26). Jesus promises the Holy Spirit (Counselor) after He "leaves." The Holy Spirit will live in the believer.
12. John 15:26,27. The Holy Spirit's coming will witness to Jesus (because the Spirit comes as Jesus promised).

NOTES

APPENDIX B / HOLY SPIRIT ······························

13. John 16:7. Jesus again confirms He must "go" before the Holy Spirit will come to His followers.
14. John 16:8-11. The Holy Spirit will convince of sin, righteousness, and judgment.
15. John 16:13. The Holy Spirit is to teach, guide, speak, reveal, and to glorify Jesus.
16. Luke 24:44-49, Acts 1:4-5. Jesus summarizes His mission and instructs followers to stay in Jerusalem to receive the Holy Spirit.
17. Acts 1:6-8. The Holy Spirit will give the necessary power to fulfill the Apostolic mission-telling the good news about God. Proof of Jesus' position as Messiah continues in each age. The Holy Spirit comes to those who ask, just as Jesus promised (Item 11).
18. Acts 2:1-4. Pentecost (Feast of Weeks, fifty days after Passover), the Holy Spirit falls on 120(?), (Acts 1:15; 2:1) like the wind, Acts 2:2 (Gen. 1:2) and Acts 2:3, like tongues of fire (Item 1).
19. Acts 2:4-13. When baptized with the Holy Spirit, Jesus' followers spoke in other languages *"as the Holy Spirit gave them utterance."*
20. Acts 2:13. Those baptized with the Holy Spirit appeared to be drunk.
21. Acts 2:14-41. The Holy Spirit emboldened Peter and led him through the first Christian sermon. Peter also gave the first Christian "altar call" and about 3,000 were baptized into fellowship (the "ekklesia").
22. Acts 2:38,39. Peter promises the Holy Spirit to all after forgiveness and baptism.
23. Acts 2:43. The Apostles began to have a miracle ministry as did Jesus, resulting from the Holy Spirit's works (Acts 19:11,12).
24. Acts 4:1-22. Peter and John healed and preached through the power of the Holy Spirit.
25. Acts 4:23-31. The Holy Spirit gave preaching boldness and effective .

NOTES

APPENDIX B / HOLY SPIRIT ·······························

26. Acts 8:14-24; 10:30-48 (esp. 10:44). The Holy Spirit is given to those who hear about Him and truly yearn to be baptized with the Holy Spirit.

27. Acts 9:1-19. Paul struck down on the road to Damascus, received the Holy Spirit through Ananias, and could then bear witness to Jesus as Christ (Acts 9:20).

28. Acts 19:1-7. The Holy Spirit baptism is more than, and different from, water baptism. Paul laid hands on some who were water baptized, but not Spirit baptized. Then the Holy Spirit came upon them.

29. Ephesians 5:15-20. Paul commands us to be filled with the Holy Spirit and not with alcohol spirits.

30. 1 Corinthians 12:1-31 (esp. 4-11). Paul lists spiritual gifts we can expect from the Holy Spirit.

31. Galatians 5:16-24 (esp. 22,23). Paul lists the fruit of the Spirit—the new nature of a person who is baptized by the Holy Spirit.

32. Luke 11:9-13. Jesus promises the Holy Spirit will be given to any who asks for it.

33. 1 Corinthians 14:1-37 (esp. 39,40). Paul teaches about orderly use of the Spirit's gifts.

34. 1 Thessalonians 5:16-22. Paul teaches the Holy Spirit should never be "quenched," but always tested for validity.

35. To receive the Holy Spirit, read *God 101* and believe item 32 above. Do not be surprised at any expression of God's power you may experience. Do not be surprised if you speak in an unknown language (tongue).

122

NOTES

APPENDIX C / CULTS ···

At the beginning of the Bible is the story of Adam, Eve, and their relationship with God. Their bliss abruptly ends with temptation followed by rebellion. They wanted to be like God and know everything (Gen. 2:17 and 3:5). The story tells how they ate of the fruit of knowledge of good and evil and were expelled from fellowship with God.

A major point illustrated here is the human need to know everything. Many people study diligently to learn all that can be known. Those who outrun others in collecting and remembering information eagerly display their knowledge. Because knowledge often precedes wisdom, many assume those two are the same. Wisdom is our proper use of knowledge, and not simply displaying it.

Alongside the hunger for knowledge is pride, a universal human flaw. Pride causes people to imagine they really are the most important and wisest, in any opinion contest. The less one knows about the vastness of human thinking and experience, the more likely he or she is to believe they have found indisputable truths and final answers.

Pride and ignorance lead the cult mind to base its religion on what it knows, instead of on who it knows. Discussion and debate of beliefs replaces praise, worship and fellowship with God. Ignorant of experiences contradicting their "true and final answer," cultists harden their beliefs and tighten their religious system. Their pride and ignorance shut them off from further inquiry. Blinded to their flaws, they are convinced they are superior people, God's truly chosen.

Articulate and attractive leaders expound their peculiar beliefs and draw more followers to their cause. Where there was once only one "true believer," now there are two. Two expands to four, and four to six. Soon there is a large body of "believers." Proselytizing, hostility, harassment, and turmoil easily follow. Rigidly holding on to their beliefs, cultists are blind to evidence that contradicts them.

NOTES

APPENDIX C / CULTS ································

True religion depends on your relationship with God; who you know, not what you know. You receive God's grace because of His perfect love, not because of perfect theology or superior knowledge. False prophets reverse God's program and require you to accept their beliefs as the only "true" way to God. It is as if they are saying, "Our way is the only way."

NOTES

APPENDIX D / BLINDERS ··

God rewards us when we recognize, confess, and repent (regret/mourn) our ignorance. The first and third Beatitudes confirm that promise (Matt. 5:3,5). The problem most people have is recognizing their ignorance before it leads to disastrous consequences. Once we know we have done something dumb, and suffer from the mistake we can repent (mourn) our ignorance.

If we could realize our intellectual deficiencies in advance of our calamity, we would rush to get whatever information we lack. But, we are blind to our own faults. Why is that? Why can't we see ourselves more clearly and minister to our own needs?

It seems there are two reasons. First, we are born ignorant. Lacking information, we must accumulate facts from experience. Experience includes both what we are taught by others and also what we learn on our own—by ourselves.

Learning is a fun facet of human nature. We all enjoy doing it. We just don't enjoy learning which requires hard disciplined study. We prefer education from easy and entertaining visual aids.

Why, then, when learning is fun, do we often find ourselves refusing to learn? There are times when our minds are closed to new ideas. Why did you wait so long to look seriously into the nature of God?

The second reason for our spiritual blinding is that Satan does not want us to understand the greater things of God. If we are blind to God's truth, or refuse to look past what we already know, we get no more blessings.

Paul explained this in his second letter to the Corinthians, chapter 4, verses 3-5 (RSV). *"In their case the god of this world has blinded the eyes of the unbelievers, to keep them from seeing the light of the gospel of the glory of Christ, who is the likeness of God."*

We must resolve to keep our minds open to new revelations from God. Our minds must be set on, "I don't want to miss anything God has for me. I shall look for His hand and mind in all things, at all times."